I0177536

HISTORIC DOUBTS RELATIVE TO NAPOLEON BONAPARTE

by

RICHARD WHATELY

Archbishop of Dublin
Author of "Elements of Logic."

HISTORIC DOUBTS RELATIVE TO NAPOLEON BONAPARTE

by

RICHARD WHATELY

Archbishop of Dublin
Author of "Elements of Logic."

Suzeteo Enterprises

Historic Doubts Relative to Napoleon Bonaparte
   By Richard Whately

Originally published in 1818. This Longmans, Green, and Co edition is from 1860.

This work is in the public domain.

Read the text online at: www.apologeticslibrary.com

Published by Suzeteo Enterprises: www.suzeteo.com

Also available in e-book formats.

ISBN: 978-1-936830-01-5

Note about the text: this work retains the spelling and phrasings that were the norm in the 1800s in England. These Anglicisms add to the reading experience. Whately's manner of citing reference works were also kept. Original capitalizations are his, as well as any italicized text. Only small adjustments here and there were made as seemed absolutely necessary. For example, Whately spelled 'Bonaparte' as 'Buonaparte.' This has been maintained in the text but changed in the title to reflect modern usage.

This edition comes with a useful index.

Table of Contents

Is not the same reason available in theology and in politics? ... Will you follow truth but to a certain point?—Burke's *Vindication of Natural Society.*

The first author who stated fairly the connexion between the evidence of testimony and the evidence of experience, was Hume, in his Essay on Miracles; a work *abounding in maxims of great use* in the conduct of life.— *Edinburgh Review*, Sept. 1814, p. 328.

PREFACE

Several of the readers of this little work (first published in 1819) have derived much amusement from the mistakes of others respecting its nature and object. It has been by some represented as a serious attempt to inculcate universal scepticism; while others have considered it as a *jeu d'esprit*, etc.[1] The author does not, however, design to entertain his readers with accounts of the mistakes which, have arisen respecting it; because many of them, he is convinced, would be received with incredulity; and he could not, without an indelicate exposure of individuals, verify his anecdotes.

But some sensible readers have complained of the difficulty of determining *what* they are to believe. Of the existence of Buonaparte, indeed, they remained fully convinced; nor, if it were left doubtful, would any important results ensue; but if they can give no *satisfactory reason* for

---

[1] It was observed by some reviewer, that Hume himself, had he been alive, would doubtless have highly enjoyed the joke! But even those who have the greatest delight in ridicule, do not relish jokes at *their own expense*. Hume may have inwardly laughed, while mystifying his readers with arguments which he himself perceived to be futile. But he did not mean the readers to perceive this. And it is not likely that he would have been amused at seeing his own fallacies exposed and held up to derision.

their conviction, how can they know, it is asked, that they may not be mistaken as to other points of greater consequence, on which they are no less fully convinced, but on which all men are *not* agreed? The author has accordingly been solicited to endeavour to frame some canons which may furnish a standard for determining what evidence is to be received.

This he conceives to be impracticable, except to that extent to which it is accomplished by a sound system of Logic; including under that title, a portion—that which relates to the *Laws of Evidence*—of what is sometimes treated under the head of "Rhetoric." But the full and complete accomplishment of such an object would confer on Man the unattainable attribute of infallibility.

But the difficulty complained of, he conceives to arise, in many instances, from men's *misstating the grounds of their own conviction*. They are convinced, indeed, and perhaps with very sufficient reason; but they imagine this reason to be a different one from what it is. The evidence to which they have assented is applied to their minds in a different manner from that in which they believe that it is—and suppose that it ought to be—applied. And when challenged to defend and justify their own belief, they feel at a loss, because they are attempting to maintain a position which is not, in fact, that in which their force lies.

For a development of the nature, the consequences, and the remedies of this mistake, the reader is referred to *Hinds on Inspiration,* pp. 30-46. If such a development is to be found in any earlier works, the Author of the following pages at least has never chanced to meet with any attempt of the kind.[2]

It has been objected, again, by some persons of no great logical accuracy of thought, that as there would not be any *moral blame* imputable to one who should seriously disbelieve, or doubt, the existence of Buonaparte, so neither is a rejection of the Scripture-histories to be considered as implying anything morally culpable.

The same objection, such as it is, would apply equally to many of the Parables of the New Testament. It might be said, for instance, that as a woman who should decline taking the trouble of searching for her lost "piece of silver," or a merchant who should neglect making an advantageous purchase of a "goodly pearl," would be guilty of no moral wrong, it must follow that there is nothing morally wrong in neglecting to reclaim a lost sinner, or in rejecting the Gospel, etc.

---

[2] See *Elements of Rhetoric*, p. i. ch. 2, § 4.

But any man of common sense readily perceives that the force of these parables consists in the circumstance that men do *not* usually show this carelessness about temporal goods; and, therefore, are guilty of gross and culpable *inconsistency*, if they are comparatively careless about what is far more important.

So, also, in the present case. If any man's mind were so constituted as to reject the same evidence in *all* matters alike—if, for instance, he really doubted or disbelieved the existence of Buonaparte, and considered the Egyptian pyramids as fabulous, because, forsooth, he had no "experience" of the erection of such huge structures, and *had* experience of travellers telling huge lies—he would be regarded, perhaps, as very silly, or as insane, but not as morally culpable. But if (as is intimated in the concluding sentence of this work) a man is influenced in one case by objections which, in another case, he would deride, then he stands convicted of being unfairly biased by his prejudices.

It is only necessary to add, that as this work first appeared in the year 1819, many things are spoken of in the present tense, to which the past would now be applicable.

Postscripts have been added to successive editions in reference to subsequent occurrences.

d

HISTORIC DOUBTS RELATIVE TO NAPOLEON BUONAPARTE.

Long as the public attention has been occupied by the extraordinary personage from whose ambition we are supposed to have so narrowly escaped, the subject seems to have lost scarcely anything of its interest. We are still occupied in recounting the exploits, discussing the character, inquiring into the present situation, and even conjecturing as to the future prospects of Napoleon Buonaparte.

Nor is this at all to be wondered at, if we consider the very extraordinary nature of those exploits, and of that character; their greatness and extensive importance, as well as the unexampled strangeness of the events, and also that strong additional stimulant, the mysterious uncertainty that hangs over the character of the man. If it be doubtful whether any history (exclusive of such as is confessedly fabulous) ever attributed to its hero such a series of wonderful achievements compressed into so small a space of time, it is certain that to no one were ever assigned so many dissimilar characters.

It is true, indeed, that party-prejudices have drawn a favourable and an unfavourable portrait of almost every eminent man; but amidst all the diversities of colouring, something of the same general outline is always distinguishable. And even the virtues in the one description bear some resemblance to the vices of another: rashness, for instance, will be called courage, or courage, rashness; heroic firmness, and obstinate pride, will correspond in the two opposite descriptions; and in some leading features both will agree. Neither the friends nor the enemies of Philip of Macedon, or of Julius Cæsar, ever questioned their COURAGE, or their MILITARY SKILL.

With Buonaparte, however, it has been otherwise. This obscure Corsican adventurer, a man, according to some, of extraordinary talents and courage, according to others, of very moderate abilities, and a rank coward, advanced rapidly in the French army, obtained a high command, gained a series of important victories, and, elated by success, embarked in an expedition against Egypt; which was planned and conducted, according to some, with the most consummate skill, according to others, with the utmost wildness and folly: he was unsuccessful, however; and leaving the army in Egypt in a very distressed situation, he returned to France, and found the nation, or at least the army, so favourably disposed towards him, that he was enabled, with the utmost ease, to overthrow the existing government, and obtain for himself the supreme power; at first, under the modest appellation of Consul, but afterwards with the more sounding title of Emperor. While in possession of this power, he overthrew the most powerful coalitions of the other European States against him; and though driven from the sea by the British fleets, overran nearly the whole continent, triumphant; finishing a war, not unfrequently, in a single campaign, he entered the capitals of most of the hostile potentates, deposed and created Kings at his pleasure, and appeared the virtual sovereign of the chief part of the continent, from the frontiers of Spain to those of Russia. Even those countries we find him invading with prodigious armies, defeating their forces, penetrating to their capitals, and threatening their total subjugation. But at Moscow his progress is stopped: a winter of unusual severity, co-operating with the efforts of the Russians, totally destroys his enormous host: and the German sovereigns throw off the yoke, and combine to oppose him. He raises another vast army, which is also ruined at Leipsic; and again another, with which, like a second Antæus, he for some time maintains himself in France; but is finally defeated, deposed, and banished to the island of Elba, of which the sovereignty is conferred on him. Thence he returns, in about nine months, at the head of 600 men, to attempt the deposition of King Louis, who had been peaceably recalled; the French nation declare in his favour, and he is reinstated without a struggle. He raises another great army to oppose the allied powers, which is totally defeated at Waterloo; he is a second time deposed, surrenders to the British, and is placed in confinement at the island of St. Helena. Such is the outline of the eventful history presented to us; in the detail of which, however, there is almost every conceivable variety of statement; while the motives and conduct of the chief actor are involved in still greater doubt, and the subject of still more eager controversy.

In the midst of these controversies, the preliminary question, concerning the *existence* of this extraordinary personage, seems never to have occurred to any one as a matter of doubt; and to show even the smallest hesitation in admitting it, would probably be regarded as an excess of scepticism; on the ground that this point has always been taken for granted by the disputants on all sides, being indeed implied by the very nature of their disputes.

But is it in fact found that *undisputed* points are always such as have been the most carefully examined as to the evidence on which they rest? that facts or principles which are taken for granted, without controversy, as the common basis of opposite opinions, are always themselves established on sufficient grounds? On the contrary, is not any such fundamental point, from the very circumstance of its being taken for granted at once, and the attention drawn off to some other question, likely to be admitted on insufficient evidence, and the flaws in that evidence overlooked?

Experience will teach us that such instances often occur: witness the well-known anecdote of the Royal Society; to whom King Charles II. proposed as a question, whence it is that a vessel of water receives no addition of weight from a live fish being put into it, though it does, if the fish be dead. Various solutions, of great ingenuity, were proposed, discussed, objected to, and defended; nor was it till they had been long bewildered in the inquiry, that it occurred to them *to try the experiment*; by which they at once ascertained that the phenomenon which they were striving to account for,—which was the acknowledged basis and substratum, as it were, of their debates,—had no existence but in the invention of the witty monarch.[3]

---

[3] "A report is spread, (says Voltaire in one of his works,) that there is, in some country or other, a giant as big as a mountain; and men presently fall to hot disputing concerning the precise length of his nose, the breadth of his thumb, and other particulars, and anathematize each other for heterodoxy of belief concerning them. In the midst of all, if some bold sceptic ventures to hint a doubt as to the existence of this giant, all are

Another instance of the same kind is so very remarkable that I cannot forbear mentioning it. It was objected to the system of Copernicus when first brought forward, that if the earth turned on its axis, as he represented, a stone dropped from the summit of a tower would not fall at the foot of it, but at a great distance to the west; *in the same manner as a stone dropped from the mast-head of a ship in full sail, does not fall at the foot of the mast, but towards the stern.* To this it was answered, that a stone being a *part* of the earth obeys the same laws, and moves with it; whereas, it is no part of the ship; of which, consequently, its motion is independent. This solution was admitted by some, but opposed by others; and the controversy went on with spirit; nor was it till *one hundred years* after the death of Copernicus, that the experiment being tried, it was ascertained that the stone thus dropped from the head of the mast *does* fall at the foot of it![4]

Let it be observed that I am not now impugning any one particular narrative; but merely showing generally, that what is *unquestioned* is not necessarily unquestionable;

---

ready to join against him, and tear him to pieces." This looks almost like a prophetic allegory relating to the gigantic Napoleon.

[4] Οὕτως ἀταλαίπωρος τοῖς πολλοῖς ἡ ζήτησις τῆς ἀληθείας, καὶ ἐπὶ τὰ ἕτοιμα μᾶλλον τρέπονται. Thucyd. b.i.c. 20.

since men will often, at the very moment when they are accurately sifting the evidence of some disputed point, admit hastily, and on the most insufficient grounds, what they have been accustomed to see taken for granted.

The celebrated Hume[5] has pointed out, also, the readiness with which men believe, on very slight evidence, any story that pleases their imagination by its admirable and marvellous character. Such hasty credulity, however, as he well remarks, is utterly unworthy of a philosophical mind; which should rather suspend its judgment the more, in proportion to the strangeness of the account, and yield to none but the most decisive and unimpeachable proofs.

Let it, then, be allowed us, as is surely reasonable, just to inquire, with respect to the extraordinary story I have been speaking of, on what evidence we believe it. We shall be told that it is *notorious*; i.e., in plain English, it is very *much talked about*. But as the generality of those who talk about Buonaparte do not even pretend to speak from *their own authority*, but

---

[5] "With what greediness are the miraculous accounts of travellers received, their descriptions of sea and land monsters, their relations of wonderful adventures, strange men, and uncouth manners!"—*Hume's Essay on Miracles*, p. 179, 12mo; p. 185, 8vo, 1767; p. 117, 8vo, 1817.

N.B.—In order to give every possible facility of reference, three editions of Hume's Essays have been generally employed: a 12mo, London, 1756, and two 8vo editions.

merely to repeat what they have casually heard, we cannot reckon them as, in any degree, witnesses; but must allow ninety-nine hundredths of what we are told to be mere hearsay, which would not be at all the more worthy of credit even if it were repeated by ten times as many more. As for those who profess to have *personally known* Napoleon Buonaparte, and to have *themselves witnessed* his transactions, I write not for them. *If any such there be*, who are inwardly conscious of the truth of all they relate, I have nothing to say to them, but to beg that they will be tolerant and charitable towards their neighbours, who have not the same means of ascertaining the truth, and who may well be excused for remaining doubtful about such extraordinary events, till most unanswerable proofs shall be adduced. "I would not have believed such a thing, if I had not seen it," is a common preface or appendix to a narrative of marvels; and usually calls forth from an intelligent hearer the appropriate answer, "*no more will I.*"

Let us, however, endeavour to trace up some of this hearsay evidence as far towards its source as we are able. Most persons would refer to the *newspapers* as the authority from which their knowledge on the subject was derived; so that, generally speaking, we may say it is on the testimony of the newspapers that men believe in the existence and exploits of Napoleon Buonaparte.

It is rather a remarkable circumstance, that it is common to hear Englishmen speak of the impudent fabrications of foreign newspapers, and express wonder that any one can be found to credit them; while they conceive that, in this favoured land, the liberty of the press is a sufficient security for veracity. It is true they often speak contemptuously of such "newspaper-stories" as last but a short time; indeed they continually see them contradicted within a day or two in the same paper, or their falsity detected by some journal of an opposite party; but still whatever is *long adhered to* and often *repeated*, especially if it also appear in *several different* papers (and this, though they notoriously copy from one another), is almost sure to be generally believed. Whence this high respect which is practically paid to newspaper authority? Do men think, that because a witness has been perpetually detected in falsehood, he may therefore be the more safely believed whenever he is *not* detected? or does adherence to a story, and frequent repetition of it, render it the more credible? On the contrary, is it not a common remark in other cases, that a liar will generally stand to and reiterate what he has once said, merely because he *has* said it?

Let us, if possible, divest ourselves of this superstitious veneration for everything that appears "in print," and examine a little more systematically the evidence which is adduced.

I suppose it will not be denied that the three following are among the most important points to be ascertained, in deciding on the credibility of witnesses; first, whether they have the means of gaining correct *information*; secondly, whether they have any *interest* in concealing truth, or propagating falsehood; and, thirdly, whether they *agree* in their testimony. Let us examine the present witnesses upon all these points.

First, what means have the editors of newspapers for giving correct information? We know not, except from their own statements. Besides what is copied from other journals, foreign or British, (which is usually more than three-fourths of the news published,)[6] they

---

[6] "Suppose a fact to be transmitted through twenty persons; the first communicating it to the second, the second to the third, etc., and let the probability of each testimony be expressed by nine-tenths, (that is, suppose that of ten reports made by each witness, nine only are true,) then, at every time the story passes from one witness to another, the evidence is reduced to nine-tenths of what it was before. Thus, after it has passed through the whole

profess to refer to the authority of certain "private correspondents" abroad; *who* these correspondents are, what means they have of obtaining information, or whether they exist at all, we have no way of ascertaining. We find ourselves in the condition of the Hindoos, who are told by their priests that the earth stands on an elephant, and the elephant on a tortoise; but are left to find out for themselves what the tortoise stands on, or whether it stands on anything at all.

So much for our clear knowledge of the means of *information* possessed by these witnesses; next, for the grounds on which we are to calculate on their *veracity*.

Have they not a manifest interest in circulating the wonderful accounts of Napoleon Buonaparte and his achievements, whether true or false? Few would read newspapers if they did not sometimes find wonderful or important news

---

twenty, the evidence will be found to be less than one-eighth."— La Place, *Essai Philosophique sur les Probabilités*.

That is, the chances for the fact thus attested being true, will be, according to this distinguished calculator, less than one in eight. Very few of the common newspaper-stories, however, relating to foreign countries, could be traced, if the matter were carefully investigated, up to an actual eye-witness, even through twenty intermediate witnesses; and many of the steps of our ladder, would, I fear, prove but rotten; few of the reporters would deserve to have *one in ten* fixed as the proportion of their false accounts.

11

in them; and we may safely say that no subject was ever found so inexhaustibly interesting as the present.

It may be urged, however, that there are several adverse political parties, of which the various public prints are respectively the organs, and who would not fail to expose each other's fabrications.[7] Doubtless they would, if they could do so without at the same time exposing *their own*; but identity of interests may induce a community of operations up to a certain point. And let it be observed that the object of contention between these rival parties is, *who* shall have the administration of public affairs, the control of public expenditure, and the disposal of places: the question, I say, is, not whether the people shall be governed or not, but, *by which party* they shall be governed;—not whether the taxes shall be paid or not, but *who* shall *receive* them. Now, it must be admitted that Buonaparte is a political bugbear, most convenient to *any* administration: "if you do not adopt our measures and reject those of our opponents, Buonaparte will be sure to prevail

---

[7] "I did not mention the difficulty of detecting a falsehood in any private or even public history, at the time and place where it is said to happen; much more where the scene is removed to ever so small a distance.... But the matter never comes to any issue, if trusted to the common method of altercation and debate and flying rumours."—*Hume's Essay on Miracles*, p. 195, 12mo; pp. 200, 201, 8vo, 1767; p. 127, 8vo, 1817.

over you; if you do not submit to the Government, at least under *our* administration, this formidable enemy will take advantage of your insubordination, to conquer and enslave you: pay your taxes cheerfully, or the tremendous Buonaparte will take all from you." Buonaparte, in short, was the burden of every song; his redoubted name was the charm which always succeeded in unloosing the purse-strings of the nation. And let us not be too sure,[8] safe as we now think ourselves, that some occasion may not occur for again producing on the stage so useful a personage: it is not merely to children in the nursery that the threat of being "given to Buonaparte" has proved effectual.

It is surely probable, therefore, that, with an object substantially the same, all parties may have availed themselves of one common instrument. It is not necessary to suppose that for this purpose they secretly entered into a formal agreement; though, by the way, there are reports afloat, that the editors of the *Courier* and *Morning Chronicle* hold amicable consultations as to the conduct of their public warfare: I will not take upon me to say that this is incredible; but at any rate it is not necessary for the establishment of the probability I contend for. Neither again would I imply that *all* newspaper

---

[8] See the third Postscript appended to this edition.

editors are utterers of forged stories, "knowing them to be forged;" most likely the great majority of them publish what they find in other papers with the same simplicity that their readers peruse it; and therefore, it must be observed, are not at all more proper than their readers to be cited as authorities.

Still it will be said, that unless we suppose a regularly preconcerted plan, we must at least expect to find great discrepancies in the accounts published. Though they might adopt the general outline of facts from one another, they would have to fill up the detail for themselves; and in this, therefore, we should meet with infinite and irreconcilable variety.

Now this is precisely the point I am tending to; for the fact exactly accords with the above supposition; the discordance and mutual contradictions of these witnesses being such as would alone throw a considerable shade of doubt over their testimony. It is not in minute circumstances alone that the discrepancy appears, such as might be expected to appear in a narrative substantially true; but in very great and leading transactions, and such as are very intimately connected with the supposed hero. For instance, it is by no means agreed whether Buonaparte led in person the celebrated charge over the bridge of Lodi, (for *celebrated* it certainly is, as well as the siege of Troy, whether either event ever really took place or no,) or was safe in the rear, while Augereau performed the exploit. The same doubt hangs over the charge of the French cavalry at Waterloo. The peasant Lacoste, who professed to have been Buonaparte's guide on the day of battle, and who earned a fortune by detailing over and over again to visitors all the particulars of what the great man said and did up to the moment of flight,—this same Lacoste has been suspected by others, besides me, of having never even been near the great man, and having fabricated the whole story for the sake of making a gain of the credulity of travellers. In the accounts that are the extant of the battle itself, published by persons professing to have been present, the reader will find that there is a discrepancy of *three or four hours* as to the time when the battle began!—a battle, be it remembered, not fought with javelins and arrows, like those of the ancients, in which one part of a large army might be engaged, whilst a distant portion of the same army knew nothing of it; but a battle commencing (if indeed it were ever fought at all) with the *firing of cannon*, which, would have announced pretty loudly what was going on.

It is no less uncertain whether or no this strange personage poisoned in Egypt an hospital—full of his own soldiers, and butchered in cold blood a garrison that had surrendered. But not to multiply instances; the battle of Borodino, which is represented as one of the greatest ever fought, was unequivocally claimed as a victory by both parties; nor is the question decided at this day. We have official accounts on both sides, circumstantially detailed, in the names of supposed respectable persons, professing to have been present on the spot; yet totally irreconcilable. *Both* these accounts *may* be false; but since *one* of them *must* be false, that one (it is no matter *which* we suppose) proves incontrovertibly this important maxim: that *it is possible for a narrative—however circumstantial—however steadily maintained—however public, and however important, the events it relates—however grave the authority on which it is published—to be nevertheless an entire fabrication!*

Many of the events which have been recorded were probably believed much the more readily and firmly, from the apparent caution and hesitation with which they were at first published—the vehement contradiction in our papers of many pretended French accounts—and the abuse lavished upon them for falsehood, exaggeration, and gasconade. But is it not possible—is it not, indeed, perfectly natural—that the publishers even of known falsehood should assume this cautious demeanour, and this abhorrence of exaggeration, in order the more easily to gain credit? Is it not also very possible, that those who actually believed what they published, may have suspected mere *exaggeration* in stories which were entire *fictions*? Many men have that sort of simplicity, that they think themselves quite secure against being deceived, provided they believe only *part* of the story they hear; when perhaps the whole is equally false. So that perhaps these simple-hearted editors, who were so vehement against lying bulletins, and so wary in announcing their great news, were in the condition of a clown, who thinks he has bought a great bargain of a Jew because he has beat down the price perhaps from a guinea to a crown, for some article that is not really worth a groat.

With respect to the *character* of Buonaparte, the dissonance is, if possible, still greater. According to some, he was a wise, humane, magnanimous hero; others paint him as a monster of cruelty, meanness, and perfidy: some, even of those who are most inveterate against him, speak very highly of his political and military ability: others place him on the very verge of insanity. But allowing that all this may be the colouring of party-prejudice, (which surely is allowing a great deal,) there is one point to which such a solution will hardly apply: if there be anything that can be clearly ascertained in history, one would think it must be the *personal courage of a military man*; yet here we are as much at a loss as ever; at the very same times, and on the same occasions, he is described by different writers as a man of undaunted intrepidity, and as an absolute poltroon.

What, then, are we to believe? If we are disposed to credit all that is told us, we must believe in the existence not only of one, but of two or three Buonapartes; if we admit nothing but what is well authenticated, we shall be compelled to doubt of the existence of any.[9]

It appears, then, that those on whose testimony the existence and actions of Buonaparte are generally believed, fail in ALL the most essential points on which the credibility of witnesses depends: first, we have no assurance that they have access to correct information; secondly, they have an apparent interest in propagating falsehood; and, thirdly, they palpably contradict each other in the most important points.

---

[9] "We entertain a suspicion concerning any matter of fact, when the witnesses *contradict* each other; when they are of a *suspicious* character; when they have an *interest* in what they affirm."—*Hume's Essay on Miracles*, p. 172, 12mo; p. 176, 8vo, 1767; p. 113, 8vo. 1817.

Another circumstance which throws additional suspicion on these tales is, that the whig-party, as they are called—the warm advocates for liberty, and opposers of the encroachments of monarchical power—have for some time past strenuously espoused the cause and vindicated the character of Buonaparte, who is represented by all as having been, if not a tyrant, at least an absolute despot. One of the most forward in this cause is a gentleman, who once stood foremost in holding up this very man to public execration—who first published, and long maintained against popular incredulity, the accounts of his atrocities in Egypt. Now that such a course should be adopted for party-purposes; by those who are aware that the whole story is a fiction, and the hero of it imaginary, seems not very incredible; but if they believed in the real existence of this despot, I cannot conceive how they could so forsake their principles as to advocate his cause, and eulogize his character.

Besides the many strange and improbable circumstances in the history of Buonaparte that have been already noticed, there are many others, two of which it may be worth while to advert to.

One of the most incredible is the received account of the persons known as the "Détenus."

It is well known that a great number of English gentlemen passed many years, in the early part of the present century, abroad;—by their own account, in France. Their statement was, that while travelling in that country for their amusement, as peaceable tourists, they were, on the sudden breaking out of a war, seized by this terrible Buonaparte, and kept prisoners for about twelve years, contrary to all the usages of civilized nations—to all principles of justice, of humanity, of enlightened policy; many of them thus wasting in captivity the most important portion of their lives, and having all their prospects blighted.

Now whether these persons were in reality exiles by choice, for the sake of keeping out of the way of creditors, or of enjoying the society of those they preferred to their own domestic circle, I do not venture to conjecture. But let the reader consider whether *any* conjecture can be *more* improbable than the statement actually made.

It is, indeed, credible that ambition may prompt an unscrupulous man to make the most enormous sacrifices of human life, and to perpetrate the most atrocious crimes, for the advancement of his views of conquest. But that this *great* man—as he is usually reckoned even by adversaries—this hero according to some—this illustrious warrior, and mighty sovereign—

should have stooped to be guilty of an act of mean and petty malice worthy of a spiteful old woman,—a piece of paltry cruelty which could not at all conduce to his success in the war, or produce any effect except to degrade his country, and exasperate ours;—this, surely, is quite incredible. "Pizarro," says Elvira in Kotzebue's play, "if not always justly, at least act always greatly."

But a still more wonderful circumstance connected with this transaction remains behind. A large portion of the English nation, and among these the whole of the Whig party, are said to have expressed the most vehement indignation, mingled with compassion, at the banishment from Europe, and confinement in St. Helena, of this great man. No considerations of regard for the peace and security of our own country, no dread of the power of so able and indefatigable a warrior, and so inveterate an enemy, should have induced us, they thought, to subject this formidable personage to a confinement, which was far less severe than that to which he was said to have subjected such numbers of our countrymen, the harmless *non-belligerent* travellers, whom (according to the story) he kidnapped in France, with no object but to gratify the basest and most unmanly spite.

But that there is no truth in that story, and that it was not believed by those who manifested so much sympathy and indignation on this great man's account, is sufficiently proved by that very sympathy and indignation.

There are again other striking improbabilities connected with the Polish nation in the history before us. Buonaparte is represented as having always expressed the strongest sympathy with that ill-used people; and they, as being devotedly attached to him, and fighting with the utmost fidelity and bravery in his armies, in which some of them attained high commands. Now he had it manifestly in his power at one period (according to the received accounts), with a stroke of his pen, to re-establish Poland as an independent state. For, in his last Russian war, he had complete occupation of the country (of which the population was perfectly friendly); the Russian portion of it was his by right of conquest; and Austria and Prussia, then his allies, and almost his subjects, would gladly have resigned their portions in exchange for some of the provinces they had ceded to France, and which were, to him, of little value, but, to them, important. And, indeed, Prussia was (as we are told) so thoroughly humbled and weakened that he might easily have enforced the cession of Prussian-Poland, even without any compensation. And the re-establishment of the Polish kingdom would have been as evidently politic as it was reasonable. The independence of a faithful and devoted ally, at enmity with the surrounding nations—the very nations that were the most likely to combine (as they often had done) against him,—this would have given him, at no cost, a kind of strong garrison to maintain his power, and keep his enemies in check.

Yet this most obvious step, the history tells us, he did not take; but made flattering speeches to the Poles, used their services, and did nothing for them!

This is, alone, sufficiently improbable. But we are required moreover to believe that the Poles,—instead of *execrating* this man, who had done them the unpardonable wrong of wantonly disappointing the expectations he had, for his own purposes, excited, thus adding treachery to ingratitude—instead of this, continued to the last as much devoted to him as ever, and even now idolize his memory! We are to believe, in short, that this Buonaparte, not only in his own conduct and adventures violated all the established rules of probability, but also caused all other persons, as many as came in contact with him, to act as no mortals ever did act before: may we not add, as no mortals ever did act at all?

Many other improbabilities might be added to the list, and will be found in the complete edition of that history, from which some extracts will be presently given, and which has been published (under the title of "Historic Certainties") by Aristarchus Newlight, with a learned commentary (not, indeed, adopting the views contained in these pages, but) quite equal in ingenuity to a late work on the "Hebrew Monarchy."

After all, it may be expected that many who perceive the force of these objections, will yet be loth to think it possible that they and the public at large can have been so long and so greatly imposed upon. And thus it is that the magnitude and boldness of a fraud becomes its best support. The millions who for so many ages have believed in Mahomet or Brahma, lean as it were on each other for support; and not having vigour of mind enough boldly to throw off vulgar prejudices, and dare be wiser than the multitude, persuade themselves that what so many have acknowledged must be true. But I call on those who boast their philosophical freedom of thought, and would fain tread in the steps of Hume and other inquirers of the like exalted and speculative genius, to follow up fairly and fully their own principles, and, throwing off the shackles of authority, to examine carefully the evidence of whatever is proposed to them, before they admit its truth.

That even in this enlightened age, as it is called, a whole nation may be egregiously imposed upon, even in matters which intimately concern them, may be proved (if it has not been already proved) by the following instance: it was stated in the newspapers, that, a month after the battle of Trafalgar, an English officer, who had been a prisoner of war, and was exchanged, returned to this country from France, and beginning to condole with his countrymen on the terrible *defeat* they had sustained, was infinitely astonished to learn that the battle of Trafalgar was a splendid victory. He had been assured, he said, that in that battle the English had been totally defeated; and the French were fully and universally persuaded that such was the fact. Now if this report of the belief of the French nation was *not* true, the British Public were completely imposed upon; if it *were* true, then both nations were, at the same time, rejoicing in the event of the same battle, as a signal victory to themselves; and consequently one or other, at least, of these nations must have been the dupes of their government: for if the battle was never fought at all, or was not decisive on either side, in that case *both* parties were deceived. This instance, I conceive, is absolutely demonstrative of the point in question.

"But what shall we say to the testimony of those many respectable persons who went to Plymouth on purpose, and saw Buonaparte with their own eyes? must they not trust their senses?" I would not disparage either the eyesight or the veracity of these gentlemen. I am ready to allow that they went to Plymouth for the purpose of seeing Buonaparte; nay, more, that they actually rowed out into the harbour in a boat, and came alongside of a man-of-war, on whose deck they saw a man in a cocked hat, who, *they were told*, was Buonaparte. This is the utmost point to which their testimony goes; how they ascertained that this man in the cocked hat had gone through all the marvellous and romantic adventures with which we have so long been amused, we are not told. Did they perceive in his physiognomy, his true name, and authentic history? Truly this evidence is such as country people give one for a story of apparitions; if you discover any signs of incredulity, they triumphantly show the very house which the ghost haunted, the identical dark corner where it used to vanish, and perhaps even the tombstone of the person whose death it foretold. Jack Cade's nobility was supported by the same irresistible kind of evidence: having asserted that the eldest son of Edmund Mortimer, Earl of March, was stolen by a beggar-woman, "became a bricklayer when he came to age," and was the father of the supposed Jack Cade; one of his companions confirms the story, by saying, "Sir, he made a chimney in my father's house, and the bricks are alive at this day to testify it; therefore, deny it not."

Much of the same kind is the testimony of our brave countrymen, who are ready to produce the scars they received in fighting against this terrible Buonaparte. That they fought and were wounded, they may safely testify; and probably they no less firmly *believe* what they were *told* respecting the cause in which they fought: it would have been a high breach of discipline to doubt it; and they, I conceive, are men better skilled in handling a musket, than in sifting evidence, and detecting imposture. But I defy any one of them to come forward and declare, *on his own knowledge*, what was the cause in which he fought,—under whose commands the opposed generals acted,—and whether the person who issued those commands did really perform the mighty achievements we are told of.

Let those, then, who pretend to philosophical freedom of inquiry,—who scorn to rest their opinions on popular belief, and to shelter themselves under the example of the unthinking multitude, consider carefully, each one for himself, what is the evidence proposed to himself in particular, for the existence of such a person as Napoleon Buonaparte:—I do not mean, whether there ever was a person bearing that *name*, for that is a question of no consequence; but whether any such person ever performed all the wonderful things attributed to him;—let him then weigh well the objections to that evidence, (of which I have given but a hasty and imperfect sketch,) and if he then finds it amount to anything *more* than a probability, I have only to congratulate him on his easy faith.

But the same testimony which would have great weight in establishing a thing intrinsically probable, will lose part of this weight in proportion as the matter attested is improbable; and if adduced in support of anything that is at variance with uniform experience,[10] will be rejected at once by all sound reasoners. Let us then consider what sort of a story it is that is proposed to our acceptance. How grossly contradictory are the reports of the different authorities, I have already remarked: but consider, by itself, the story told by any one of them; it carries an air of fiction and romance on the very face of it. All the events are great, and

---

[10] "That testimony itself derives all its force from experience, seems very certain.... The first author, we believe, who stated fairly the connexion between the evidence of testimony and the evidence of experience, was Hume, in his *Essay on Miracles*, a work ... abounding in maxims of great use in the conduct of life."—*Edin. Review*, Sept. 1814, p. 328.

splendid, and marvellous;[11] great armies,—great victories,—great frosts,—great reverses,—"hairbreadth 'scapes,"—empires subverted in a few days; everything happened in defiance of political calculations, and in opposition to the *experience* of past times; everything upon that grand scale, so common in Epic Poetry, so rare in real life; and thus calculated to strike the imagination of the vulgar, and to remind the sober-thinking few of the Arabian Nights. Every event, too, has that *roundness* and completeness which is so characteristic of fiction; nothing is done by halves; we have *complete* victories,— *total* overthrows, *entire* subversion of empires,—*perfect* re-establishments of them,— crowded upon us in rapid succession. To enumerate the improbabilities of each of the several parts of this history, would fill volumes; but they are so fresh in every one's memory, that there is no need of such a detail: let any judicious man, not ignorant of history and of human nature, revolve them in his mind, and consider how far they are conformable to

---

[11] "Suppose, for instance, that the fact which the testimony endeavours to establish partakes of the extraordinary and the marvellous; in that case, the evidence resulting from the testimony receives a diminution, greater or less in proportion as the fact is more or less unusual."—*Hume's Essay on Miracles*, p. 173, 12mo; p. 176, 8vo, 1767; p. 113, 8vo, 1817.

Experience,[12] our best and only sure guide. In vain will he seek in history for something similar to this wonderful Buonaparte; "nought but himself can be his parallel."

Will the conquests of Alexander be compared with his? *They* were effected over a rabble of effeminate, undisciplined barbarians; else his progress would hardly have been so rapid: witness his father Philip, who was much longer occupied in subduing the comparatively insignificant territory of the warlike and civilized Greeks, notwithstanding their being divided into numerous petty States, whose mutual jealousy enabled him to contend with them separately. But the Greeks had never made such progress in arts and arms as the great and powerful States of Europe, which Buonaparte is represented as so speedily overpowering. His empire has been compared to the Roman: mark the contrast; he gains in a few years, that dominion, or at least control, over Germany, wealthy, civilized, and powerful, which the Romans in the plenitude of their power, could not obtain, during a struggle of as many centuries, against the ignorant half-savages who then possessed it; of whom Tacitus remarks,

---

[12] "The ultimate standard by which we determine all disputes that may arise is always derived from experience and observation."—*Hume's Essay on Miracles*, p. 172, 12mo; p. 175, 8vo, 1767; p. 112, 8vo, 1817.

that, up to his own time they had been "triumphed over rather than conquered."

Another peculiar circumstance in the history of this extraordinary personage is, that when it Is found convenient to represent him as defeated, though he is by no means defeated by halves, but involved in much more sudden and total ruin than the personages of real history usually meet with; yet, if it is thought fit he should be restored, it is done as quickly and completely as if Merlin's rod had been employed. He enters Russia with a prodigious army, which is totally ruined by an unprecedented hard winter; (everything relating to this man is *prodigious* and *unprecedented*;) yet in a few months we find him intrusted with another great army in Germany, which is also totally ruined at Leipsic; making, inclusive of the Egyptian, the third great army thus totally lost: yet the French are so good-natured as to furnish him with another sufficient to make a formidable stand in France; he is, however, *conquered, and presented with the sovereignty of Elba*; (surely, by the bye, some more *probable* way might have been found of disposing of him, till again wanted, than to place him thus on the very verge of his ancient dominions;) thence he returns to France, where he is received with open arms, and enabled to lose a fifth great army at Waterloo; yet so eager were these people to be a sixth time led to destruction, that it was found necessary to confine *him* in an island some thousand miles off, and to quarter foreign troops upon *them*, lest they should make an insurrection in his favour?[13] Does any one believe all this, and yet refuse to believe a miracle? Or rather, what is this but a miracle? Is it not a violation of the laws of nature? for surely there are moral laws of nature as well as physical; which though more liable to exceptions in this or that particular case, are no less *true as general rules* than the laws of matter, and therefore cannot be violated and contradicted *beyond a certain point*, without a miracle.[14]

---

[13]   Ἢ θαύματα πολλά.
         Καί τοί τι καί βροτῶν φρένας
         ΥΠΕΡ ΤΟΝ ΑΛΗΘΗ ΛΟΓΟΝ
         Δεδειδαλμένοι ψεύδεσι ποικίλοις
         Ἐξαπατῶντι μῦθοι.—Pind. Olymp. 1

[14] This doctrine, though hardly needing confirmation from authority, is supported by that of Hume; his eighth essay is, throughout, an argument for the doctrine of "Philosophical necessity," drawn entirely from the general uniformity, observable in the course of nature with respect to the principles of *human conduct,* as well as those of the material universe; from which uniformity, he observes, it is that we are enabled *in both cases,* to form our judgment by means of *Experience:* "and if," says he, "we would explode any forgery in history, we cannot make use of a more convincing argument, than to prove that the actions ascribed to any person, are directly contrary to the course of nature...."

"... The Veracity of Quintus Curtius is as suspicious when he describes the supernatural courage of Alexander, by which he was hurried on singly to attack multitudes, as when he describes his supernatural force and activity, by which he was able to resist them. So readily and universally do we acknowledge a *uniformity in human motives and actions, as well as in the operations of body.*"—*Eighth Essay*, p. 131, 12mo; p. 85, 8vo, 1817.

Accordingly, in the tenth essay, his use of the term "miracle," after having called it "a transgression of a law of nature," plainly shows that he meant to include *human* nature: "no testimony," says he, "is sufficient to establish a miracle, unless the testimony be of such a nature that its falsehood would be more miraculous than the fact which it endeavours to establish." The term "prodigy" also (which he all along employs as synonymous with "miracle") is applied to testimony, in the same manner, immediately after; "In the foregoing reasoning we have supposed ... that the falsehood of that testimony would be a kind of *prodigy*." Now had he meant to confine the meaning of "miracle," and "prodigy," to a violation of the laws of *matter*, the epithet "*miraculous*," applied even thus hypothetically, to *false testimony*, would be as unmeaning as the epithets "green" or "square;" the only possible sense in which we can apply to it, even in imagination, the term "miraculous," is that of "highly improbable,"—"contrary to those laws of nature which respect human conduct:" and in this sense he accordingly uses the word in the very next sentence: "When any one tells me that he saw a dead man restored to life, I immediately consider with myself whether it be more *probable* that this person should either deceive or be deceived, or that the fact which he relates should really have happened. I weigh the one *miracle* against the other."—*Hume's Essay on Miracles*, pp. 176, 177, 12mo; p. 182, 8vo, 1767; p. 115, 8vo, 1817.

See also a passage above quoted from the same essay, where he speaks of "the *miraculous* accounts of travellers;" evidently using the word in this sense.

Perhaps it was superfluous to cite authority for applying the term "miracle" to whatever is "highly improbable;" but it is important to the students of Hume, to be fully aware that he uses

Nay, there is this additional circumstance which renders the contradiction of Experience more glaring in this case than in that of the miraculous histories which ingenious sceptics have held up to contempt: all the advocates of miracles admit that they are rare exceptions to the general course of nature; but contend that they must needs be so, on account of the rarity of those extraordinary *occasions* which are the *reason* of their being performed: a Miracle, they say, does not happen every day, because a Revelation is not given every day. It would be foreign to the present purpose to seek for arguments against this answer; I leave it to those who are engaged in the controversy, to find a reply to it; but my present object is, to point out that this solution does not at all apply in the present case. Where is the peculiarity of the *occasion*? What sufficient *reason* is there for a series of events occurring in the eighteenth and nineteenth centuries, which never took place before? Was Europe at that period peculiarly weak, and in a state of barbarism, that one man could achieve such conquests, and acquire such a vast empire? On the contrary, she was flourishing in the height of strength and civilization. Can the persevering attachment and

---

those two expressions as synonymous; since otherwise they would mistake the meaning of that passage which he justly calls "a general maxim worthy of your attention."

blind devotedness of the French to this man, be accounted for by his being the descendant of a long line of kings, whose race was hallowed by hereditary veneration? No; we are told he was a low-born usurper, and not even a Frenchman! Is it that he was a good and kind sovereign? He is represented not only as an imperious and merciless despot, but as most wantonly careless of the lives of his soldiers. Could the French army and people have failed to hear from the wretched survivors of his supposed Russian expedition, how they had left the corpses of above 100,000 of their comrades bleaching on the snow-drifts of that dismal country, whither his mad ambition had conducted him, and where his selfish cowardice had deserted them? Wherever we turn to seek for circumstances that may help to account for the events of this incredible story, we only meet with such as aggravate its improbability.[15] Had it been told of some distant country, at a remote period, we could not have told what peculiar circumstances there might have been to render probable what seems to us most strange; and yet in *that* case

---

[15] "Events may be so extraordinary that they can hardly be established by testimony. We would not give credit to a man who would affirm that he saw a hundred dice thrown in the air, and that they all fell on the same faces."—*Edin. Review*, Sept. 1814, p. 327. Let it be observed, that the instance here given is *miraculous* in no other sense but that of being highly *improbable*.

every philosophical sceptic, every free-thinking speculator, would instantly have rejected such a history, as utterly unworthy of credit. What, for instance, would the great Hume, or any of the philosophers of his school, have said, if they had found in the antique records of any nation, such a passage as this? "There was a certain man of Corsica, whose name was Napoleon, and he was one of the chief captains of the host of the French; and he gathered together an army, and went and fought against Egypt: but when the king of Britain heard thereof, he sent ships of war and valiant men to fight against the French in Egypt. So they warred against them, and prevailed, and strengthened the hands of the rulers of the land against the French, and drave away Napoleon from before the city of Acre. Then Napoleon left the captains and the army that were in Egypt, and fled, and returned back to France. So the French people, took Napoleon, and made him ruler over them, and he became exceeding great, insomuch that there was none like him of all that had ruled over France before."

What, I say, would Hume have thought of this, especially if he had been told that it was at this day generally credited? Would he not have confessed that he had been mistaken in supposing there was a peculiarly blind credulity and prejudice in favour of everything that is accounted *sacred*;[16] for that, since even professed sceptics swallow implicitly such a story as this, it appears there must be a still blinder prejudice in favour of everything that is *not* accounted sacred?

Suppose, again, we found in this history such passages as the following: "And it came to pass after these things that Napoleon strengthened himself, and gathered together another host instead of that which he had lost, and went and warred against the Prussians, and the Russians, and the Austrians, and all the rulers of the north country, which were confederate against him. And the ruler of Sweden, also, which was a Frenchman, warred against Napoleon. So they went forth, and fought against the French in the plain of Leipsic. And the French were discomfited before their enemies, and fled, and came to the rivers which are behind Leipsic, and essayed to pass over, that they might escape out of the hand of their enemies; but they could not, for Napoleon had broken down the bridges: so the people of the north countries came upon them, and smote them with a very grievous slaughter." ...

---

[16] "If the spirit of religion join itself to the love of wonder, there is an end of common sense; and human testimony in these circumstances loses all pretensions to authority."—*Hume's Essay on Miracles*, p. 179, 12mo; p. 185, 8vo, 1767; p. 117, 8vo, 1817.

"Then the ruler of Austria and all the rulers of the north countries sent messengers unto Napoleon to speak peaceably unto him, saying, Why should there be war between us any more? Now Napoleon had put away his wife, and taken the daughter of the ruler of Austria to wife. So all the counsellors of Napoleon came and stood before him, and said, Behold now these kings are merciful kings; do even as they say unto thee; knowest thou not yet that France is destroyed? But he spake roughly unto his counsellors, and drave them, out from his presence, neither would he hearken unto their voice. And when all the kings saw that, they warred against France, and smote it with the edge of the sword, and came near to Paris, which is the royal city, to take it: so the men of Paris went out, and delivered up the city to them. Then those kings spake kindly unto the men of Paris, saying, Be of good cheer, there shall no harm happen unto you. Then were the men of Paris glad, and said, Napoleon is a tyrant; he shall no more rule over us. Also all the princes, the judges, the counsellors, and the captains whom Napoleon had raised up even from the lowest of the people, sent unto Lewis the brother of King Lewis, whom they had slain, and made him king over France." ...

"And when Napoleon saw that the kingdom was departed from him, he said unto the rulers which came against him, Let me, I pray you, give the kingdom unto my son: but they would not hearken unto him. Then he spake yet again, saying, Let me, I pray you, go and live in the island of Elba, which is over against Italy, nigh unto the coast of France; and ye shall give me an allowance for me and my household, and the land of Elba also for a possession. So they made him ruler of Elba."...

"In those days the Pope returned unto his own land. Now the French, and divers other nations of Europe, are servants of the Pope, and hold him in reverence; but he is an abomination unto the Britons, and to the Prussians, and to the Russians, and to the Swedes. Howbeit the French had taken away all his lands, and robbed him of all that he had, and carried him away captive into France. But when the Britons, and the Prussians, and the Russians, and the Swedes, and the rest of the nations that were confederate against France, came thither, they caused the French to set the Pope at liberty, and to restore all his goods that they had taken; likewise they gave him back all his possessions; and he went home in peace, and ruled over his own city as in times past."...

"And it came to pass when Napoleon had not yet been a full year at Elba, that he said unto his men of war that clave unto him, Go to, let us go back to France, and fight against King Lewis, and thrust him out from being king. So he departed, he and six hundred men with him that drew the sword, and warred against King Lewis. Then all the men of Belial gathered themselves together, and said, God save Napoleon. And when Lewis saw that, he fled, and gat him into the land of Batavia: and Napoleon ruled over France," etc. etc. etc. [17]

Now if a free-thinking philosopher—one of those who advocate the cause of unbiassed reason, and despise pretended revelations—were to meet with such a tissue of absurdities as this in an old Jewish record, would he not reject it at once as too palpable an imposture [18] to deserve

---

[17] The supposed history from which the above extracts are given, is published entire in the work called *Historic Certainties*.

[18] "I desire any one to lay his hand upon his heart, and after serious consideration declare whether he thinks that the falsehood of such a book, supported by such testimony, would be more extraordinary and miraculous than all the miracles it relates."—*Hume's Essay on Miracles*, p. 200, 12mo; p. 206, 8vo, 1767; p. 131, 8vo, 1817.

even any inquiry into its evidence? Is that credible then of the civilized Europeans now, which could not, if reported of the semi-barbarous Jews 3000 years ago, be established by any testimony? Will it be answered, that "there is nothing *supernatural* in all this?" Why is it, then, that you object to what is *supernatural*—that you reject every account of *miracles*—if not because they are *improbable*? Surely then a story equally or still more improbable, is not to be implicitly received, merely on the ground that it is *not* miraculous: though in fact, as I have already (in note, p. 39,) shown from Hume's authority, it *is* really miraculous. The opposition to Experience has been proved to be as complete in this case, as in what are commonly called miracles; and the reasons assigned for that contrariety by the defenders of *them*, cannot be pleaded in the present instance. If then philosophers, who reject every wonderful story that is maintained by priests, are yet found ready to believe *everything else*, however improbable, they will surely lay themselves open to the accusation brought against them of being unduly prejudiced against whatever relates to religion.

Let it be borne in mind that Hume (as I have above remarked) continually employs the term "miracle" and "prodigy" to signify anything that is highly *improbable* and *extraordinary*.

There is one more circumstance which I cannot forbear mentioning, because it so much adds to the air of fiction which pervades every part of this marvellous tale; and that is, the *nationality* of it.[19]

Buonaparte prevailed over all the hostile States in turn, *except England*; in the zenith of his power, his fleets were swept from the sea, *by England*; his troops always defeat an equal, and frequently even a superior number of those of any other nation, *except the English*; and with them it is just the reverse; twice, and twice only, he is personally engaged against an *English commander*, and both times he is totally defeated; at Acre, and at Waterloo; and to crown all, *England* finally crushes this tremendous power, which had so long kept the continent in subjection or in alarm; and to the *English* he surrenders himself prisoner! Thoroughly national, to be sure! It *may* be all very true; but I would only ask, *if* a story *had* been fabricated for the express purpose of amusing the English nation, could it have been contrived more ingeniously? It would do admirably for an epic

---

[19] "The wise lend a very academic faith to every report which favours the passion of the reporter, whether it magnifies his *country*, his family, or himself."—*Hume's Essay on Miracles*, p. 144, 12mo; p. 200, 8vo, 1767; p. 126, 8vo, 1817.

poem; and indeed bears a considerable resemblance to the Iliad and the Æneid; in which Achilles and the Greeks, Æneas and the Trojans, (the ancestors of the Romans) are so studiously held up to admiration. Buonaparte's exploits seem magnified in order to enhance the glory of his conquerors; just as Hector is allowed to triumph during the absence of Achilles, merely to give additional splendour to his overthrow by the arm of that invincible hero. Would not this circumstance alone render a history rather *suspicious* in the eyes of an acute critic, even if it were not filled with such gross improbabilities; and induce him to suspend his judgment, till very satisfactory evidence (far stronger than can be found in this case) should be produced?

Is it then too much to demand of the wary academic[20] a suspension of judgment as to the "life and adventures of Napoleon Buonaparte?" I do not pretend to *decide* positively that there is not, nor ever was, any such person; but merely to propose it as a *doubtful* point, and one the more deserving of careful investigation, from the very circumstance of its having hitherto been admitted without inquiry. Far less would I

---

[20] "Nothing can be more contrary than such a philosophy (the academic or sceptical) to the supine indolence of the mind, its rash arrogance, its lofty pretensions, and its superstitious credulity."—*Fifth Essay*, p. 68, 12mo; p. 41, 8vo, 1817.

undertake to decide what is or has been the real state of affairs. He who points out the improbability of the current story, is not bound to suggest an hypothesis of his own;[21] though it may safely be affirmed, that it would be hard to invent any one more improbable than the received one. One may surely be allowed to hesitate in admitting the stories which the ancient poets tell, of earthquakes and volcanic eruptions being caused by imprisoned giants, without being called upon satisfactorily to account for those phenomena.

Amidst the defect of valid evidence under which, as I have already shown, we labour in the present instance, it is hardly possible to offer more than here and there a probable conjecture; or to pronounce how much may be true, and how much fictitious, in the accounts presented to us. For, it is to be observed that this case is much *more* open to sceptical doubts even than some miraculous histories; since some of *them* are of such a nature that you cannot consistently admit a part and reject the rest; but are bound, if you are satisfied as to the reality of any one miracle, to embrace the whole system; so that it is necessary for the sceptic to impeach the evidence of *all* of them, separately, and

---

[21] See *Hume's Essay on Miracles*, pp. 189, 191, 195, 12mo; pp. 193, 197, 201, 202, 8vo, 1767; pp. 124, 125, 126, 8vo, 1817.

collectively: whereas, *here*, each single point requires to be *established* separately, since no one of them authenticates the rest. Supposing there be a state-prisoner at St. Helena, (which, by the way, it is acknowledged many of the French disbelieve,) how do we know who he is, or why he is confined there? There have been state-prisoners before now, who were never guilty of subjugating half Europe, and whose offences have been very imperfectly ascertained. Admitting that there have been bloody wars going on for several years past, which is highly probable, it does not follow that the events of those wars were such as we have been told;—that Buonaparte was the author and conductor of them;—or that such a person ever existed. What disturbances may have taken place in the government of the French people, we, and even nineteen-twentieths of *them*, have no means of learning but from imperfect hearsay evidence; and how much credit they themselves attach to that evidence is very doubtful. This at least is certain: that a M. Berryer, a French advocate, has published memoirs, professing to record many of the events of the recent history of France, in which, among other things, he states his conviction that Buonaparte's escape from Elba was designed and contrived by the English

Government.[22] And we are assured by many travellers that this was, and is, commonly reported in France.

Now that the French should believe the whole story about Buonaparte according to this version of it, does seem utterly incredible. Let any one suppose them seriously believing that we maintained for many years a desperate struggle against this formidable emperor of theirs, in the course of which we expended such an enormous amount of blood and treasure as is reported;—that we finally, after encountering enormous risks, succeeded in subduing him, and secured him in a place of safe exile;—and that, in less than a year after, we turned him out again, like a bag-fox,—or rather, a bag-lion,— for the sake of amusing ourselves by again staking all that was dear to us on the event of a doubtful and bloody battle, in which defeat must be ruinous, and victory, if obtained at all, must cost us many thousands of our best soldiers. Let any one force himself for a moment to conceive the French seriously believing such a mass of absurdity; and the inference must be that such a people must be prepared to believe anything. They might fancy their own country to abound not only with Napoleons, but with dragons and centaurs, and "men whose heads do grow

---

[22] See *Edinburgh Review* for October, 1842, p. 162.

beneath their shoulders," or anything else that any lunatic ever dreamt of. If we could suppose the French capable of such monstrous credulity as the above supposition would imply, it is plain their testimony must be altogether worthless.

But, on the other hand, suppose them to be aware that the British Government have been all along imposing on us, and it is quite natural that they should deride our credulity, and try whether there is anything too extravagant for us to swallow. And indeed, if Buonaparte was in fact altogether a phantom conjured up by the British Ministers, then it is *true* that his escape from Elba really *was*, as well as *the rest of his exploits*, a contrivance of theirs.

But whatever may be believed by the French relative to the recent occurrences, in their own country, and whatever may be the real character of these occurrences, of this at least we are well assured, that there have been numerous bloody wars with France under the dominion of the *Bourbons*: and we are now told that France is governed by a Bourbon king, of the name of Lewis, who professes to be in the twenty-third year of his reign. Let every one conjecture for himself. I am far from pretending to decide who may have been the governor or governors of the

French nation, and the leaders of their armies, for several years past. Certain it is, that when men are indulging their inclination for the marvellous, they always show a strong propensity to accumulate upon *one* individual (real or imaginary) the exploits of many; besides multiplying and exaggerating these exploits a thousandfold. Thus, the expounders of the ancient mythology tell us there were several persons of the name of Hercules, (either originally bearing that appellation, or having it applied to them as an honour,) whose collective feats, after being dressed up in a sufficiently marvellous garb, were attributed to a single hero. Is it not just possible, that during the rage for words of Greek derivation, the title of "Napoleon," (Ναπολεων,) which signifies "Lion of the forest," may have been conferred by the popular voice on more than one favorite general, distinguished for irresistible valour? Is it not also possible that "BUONA PARTE" may have been originally a sort of cant term applied to the "good (i.e., the bravest or most patriotic) part" of the French army, collectively; and have been afterwards mistaken for the proper name of an individual?[23] I do not profess to support this

---

[23] It is well know with how much learning and ingenuity the Rationalists of the German school have laboured to throw discredit on the literal interpretation of the narratives, both of the Old and the New Testaments; representing them as MYTHS,

conjecture; but it is certain that such mistakes may and do occur. Some critics have supposed that the Athenians imagined Anastasis ("Resurrection") to be a new goddess, in whose cause Paul was preaching. Would it have been thought anything incredible if we had been told that the ancient Persians, who had no idea of any but a monarchical government, had supposed Aristocratia to be a queen of Sparta? But we need not confine ourselves to hypothetical cases; it is positively stated that the Hindoos at this day believe "the honourable East India Company" to be a venerable old lady of high dignity, residing in this country. The Germans, again, of the present day derive their name from a similar mistake: the first tribe of them who invaded Gaul[24] assumed the honourable title of "*Ger-*

---

i.e., fables allegorically describing some physical or moral phænomena—philosophical principles—systems, etc.—under the figure of actions performed by certain ideal personages; these allegories having been, afterwards, through the mistake of the vulgar, believed as history. Thus, the real historical existence of such a person as the supposed founder of the Christian religion, and the acts attributed to him, are denied in the literal sense, and the whole of the evangelical history is explained on the "mythical" theory.

Now it is a remarkable circumstance in reference to the point at present before us, that an eminent authoress of this century has distinctly declared that Napoleon Buonaparte was NOT A MAN, but a SYSTEM.

[24] Germaniæ vocabulum recens et nuper additum; quoniam qui primi Rhenum transgressi Gallos expulerint, ac nunc Tungri, tunc Germani vocati sint: ita nationis nomen in nomen gentis

man" which signifies "warriors," (the words "war" and "guerre," as well as "man," which remains in our language unaltered, are evidently derived from the Teutonic,) and the Gauls applied this as a *name* to the whole *race*.

However, I merely throw out these conjectures without by any means contending that more plausible ones might not be suggested. But whatever supposition we adopt, or whether we adopt any, the objections to the commonly received accounts will remain in their full force, and imperiously demand the attention of the candid sceptic.

I call upon those, therefore, who profess themselves advocates of free inquiry—who disdain to be carried along with the stream of popular opinion, and who will listen to no testimony that runs counter to experience,—to follow up their own principles fairly and consistently. Let the same mode of argument be adopted in all cases alike; and then it can no longer be attributed to hostile prejudice, but to enlarged and philosophical views. If they have already rejected some histories, on the ground of their being strange and marvellous,—of their relating facts, unprecedented, and at variance with the established course of nature,—let them

---

evaluisse paullatim, ut omnes, primum a victore ob metum, mox a seipsis invento nomine, Germani vocarentur.—*Tacitus, de Mor. Germ.*

not give credit to another history which lies open to the very same objections,—the extraordinary and romantic tale we have been just considering. If they have discredited the testimony of witnesses, who are *said* at least to have been disinterested, and to have braved persecutions and death in support of their assertions,—can these philosophers consistently listen to and believe the testimony of those who avowedly *get money* by the tales they publish, and who do not even pretend that they incur any serious risk in case of being detected in a falsehood? If, in other cases, they have refused to listen to an account which has passed through many intermediate hands before it reaches them, and which is defended by those who have an interest in maintaining it; let them consider through how many, and what very suspicious hands, *this* story has arrived to them, without the possibility, as I have shown, of tracing it back to any decidedly authentic source, after all;—to any better authority, according to their own showing, than that of an *unnamed* and unknown foreign correspondent;—and likewise how strong an interest, in every way, those who have hitherto imposed on them, have in keeping up the imposture. Let them, in short, show themselves as ready to detect the cheats, and despise the fables of politicians as of priests.

But if they are still wedded to the popular belief in this point, let them be consistent enough to admit the same evidence in *other* cases which they yield to in *this*. If, after all that has been said, they cannot bring themselves to doubt of the existence of Napoleon Buonaparte, they must at least acknowledge that they do not apply to that question the same plan of reasoning which they have made use of in others; and they are consequently bound in reason and in honesty to renounce it altogether.

POSTSCRIPT TO THE
THIRD EDITION.

It may seem arrogant for an obscure and nameless individual to claim the glory of having put to death the most formidable of all recorded heroes. But a shadowy champion may be overthrown by a shadowy antagonist. Many a terrific spectre has been laid by the beams of a halfpenny candle. And if I have succeeded in making out, in the foregoing pages, a probable case of suspicion, it must, I think, be admitted, that there is some ground for my present boast, of having *killed* Napoleon Buonaparte.

Let but the circumstances of the case be considered. This mighty Emperor, who had been so long the bugbear of the civilized world, after having obtained successes and undergone reverses, such as never befel any (other at least) *real* potentate, was at length sentenced to confinement in the remote island of St. Helena: a measure which many persons wondered at, and many objected to, on various grounds; not unreasonably, supposing the illustrious exile to be a real person; but on the supposition of his being only a man of straw, the situation was exceedingly favourable for keeping him out of the way of impertinent curiosity, when not wanted, and for making him the foundation of any new plots that there might be occasion to conjure up.

About this juncture it was that the public attention was first invited, by these pages, to the question as to the real existence of Napoleon Buonaparte. They excited, it may be fairly supposed, along with much surprise and much censure, some degree of doubt, and probably of consequent inquiry. No fresh evidence, as far as I can learn, of the truth of the disputed points, was brought forward to dispel these doubts. We heard, however, of the most jealous precautions being used to prevent any intercourse between the formidable prisoner, and any stranger who, from motives of curiosity, might wish to visit him. The "man in the iron mask" could hardly have been more rigorously secluded: and we also heard various contradictory reports of conversations between him and the few who were allowed access to him; the falsehood and inconsistency of most of these reports being proved in contemporary publications.

At length, just about the time when the public scepticism respecting this extraordinary personage might be supposed to have risen to an alarming height, it was announced to us that he was dead! A stop was thus put, most opportunely, to all troublesome inquiries. I do not undertake to deny that such a person did live and die. That he was, and that he did, *everything* that is reported, we cannot believe, unless we consent to admit contradictory statements; but many of the events reported, however marvellous, are certainly not, when taken separately, physically impossible. But I would only entreat the candid reader to reflect what might naturally be expected, on the supposition of the surmises contained in the present work being well founded. Supposing the whole of the tale I have been considering to have been a fabrication, what would be the natural result of such attempt to excite inquiry into its truth? Evidently the shortest and most effectual mode of avoiding detection, would be to *kill* the phantom, and so get rid of him at once. A ready and decisive answer would thus be provided to any one in whom the foregoing arguments might have excited suspicions: "Sir, there can be no doubt that such a person existed, and performed what is related of him; and if you will just take a voyage to St. Helena, you may see with your own eyes,—not him, indeed, for he is no longer living,—but his *tomb*: and what evidence would you have that is more decisive?"

So much for his *Death*: as for his *Life*,—it is just published by an eminent writer: besides which, the shops will supply us with abundance of busts and prints of this great man; all striking likenesses—of one another. The most

incredulous must be satisfied with this! "Stat magni NOMINIS umbra!"
    KONX OMPAX.

POSTSCRIPT TO THE
SEVENTH EDITION.

Since the publication of the Sixth Edition of this work, the French nation, and the world at large, have obtained an additional evidence, to which I hope they will attach as much weight as it deserves, of the reality of the wonderful history I have been treating of. The Great Nation, among the many indications lately given of an heroic zeal like what Homer attributes to his Argive warriors, τίσασθαι ἙΛἘΝΗΣ ὁρμήματά τε στοναχάς τε, have formed and executed the design of bringing home for honourable interment the remains of their illustrious Chief.

How many persons have actually inspected these relics, I have not ascertained; but that a real coffin, containing real bones, was brought from St. Helena to France, I see no reason to disbelieve.

Whether future visitors to St. Helena will be shown merely the identical *place* in which Buonaparte was (*said* to have been) interred, or whether another set of real bones will be exhibited in that island, we have yet to learn.

This latter supposition is not very improbable. It was something of a credit to the island, an attraction to strangers, and a source of profit to some of the inhabitants, to possess so remarkable a relic; and this glory and advantage they must naturally wish to retain. If so, there seems no reason why they should not have a Buonaparte of their own; for there is, I believe, no doubt that there are, or were, several Museums in England, which, among other curiosities, boasted, each, of a genuine skull of Oliver Cromwell.

Perhaps, therefore, we shall hear of several well authenticated skulls of Buonaparte also, in the collections of different virtuosos, all of whom (especially those in whose own crania the "organ of wonder" is the most largely developed) will doubtless derive equal satisfaction from the relics they respectively possess.

POSTSCRIPT TO THE NINTH EDITION.

The Public has been of late much interested and not a little bewildered, by the accounts of many strange events, said to have recently taken place in France and other parts of the Continent. Are these accounts of such a character as to allay, or to strengthen and increase, such doubts as have been suggested in the foregoing pages?

We are told that there is now a Napoleon Buonaparte at the head of the government of France. It is not, indeed, asserted that he is the very original Napoleon Buonaparte himself. The death of that personage, and the transportation of his genuine bones to France, had been too widely proclaimed to allow of his reappearance in his own proper person. But "uno avulso, non deficit alter." Like the Thibetian worshippers of the Dalai Lama, (who never dies; only his soul transmigrates into a fresh body), the French are so resolved, we are told, to be under a Buonaparte—whether that be (see note to p. 56) a man or "a system"—that they have found, it seems, a kind of new incarnation of this their Grand Lama, in a person said to be the nephew of the original one.

And when, on hearing that this personage now fills the high office of President of the French Republic, we inquire (very naturally) *how he came there*, we are informed that, several years ago, he invaded France in an English vessel, (the *English*—as was observed in p. 52—having always been suspected of keeping Buonaparte ready, like the winds in a Lapland witch's bag, to be let out on occasion,) at the head of a force, not, of six hundred men, like his supposed uncle in his expedition from Elba, but of fifty-five,(!) with which he landed at Boulogne, proclaimed himself emperor, and was joined by no less than *one* man! He was accordingly, we are told, arrested, brought to trial, and sentenced to imprisonment; but having, some years after, escaped from prison, and taken refuge in England, (*England* again!) he thence returned to France: AND SO the French nation placed him at the head of the government!

All this will doubtless be received as a very probable tale by those who have given full credit to all the stories I have alluded to in the foregoing pages.

POSTSCRIPT TO THE ELEVENTH EDITION.

When any dramatic piece *takes*—as the phrase is—with the Public, it will usually be represented again and again with still-continued applause; and sometimes imitations of it will be produced; so that the same drama in substance will, with occasional slight variations in the plot, and changes of names, long keep possession of the stage.

Something like this has taken place with respect to that curious tragi-comedy—the scene of it laid in France—which has engaged the attention of the British public for about sixty years; during which it has been "exhibited to crowded houses"—viz., coffee-houses, reading-rooms, etc., with unabated interest.

The outline of this drama, or series of dramas, may be thus sketched:

Dramatis Personæ.

A. A King or other Sovereign.

B. His Queen.

C. The Heir apparent.

D. E. F. His Ministers.

G. H. I. J. K. Demagogues.

L. A popular leader of superior ingenuity, who becomes ultimately supreme ruler under the title of Dictator, Consul, Emperor, King, President, or some other.

Soldiers, Senators, Executioners, and other functionaries, Citizens, Fishwomen, etc.

Scene, Paris.

(1.) The first Act of one of these dramas represents a monarchy, somewhat troubled by murmurs of disaffection, suspicions of conspiracy, etc.

(2.) Second Act, a rebellion; in which ultimately the government is overthrown.

(3.) Act the third, a provisional government established, on principles of liberty, equality, fraternity, etc.

(4.) Act the fourth, struggles of various parties for power, carried on with sundry intrigues, and sanguinary conflicts.

(5.) Act the fifth, the re-establishment of some form of absolute monarchy.

And from this point we start afresh, and begin the same business over again, with sundry fresh interludes.

All this is highly amusing to the English Public to *hear* and *read* of; but I doubt whether our countrymen would like to be actual *performers* in such a drama.

Whether the French really are so, or whether they are mystifying us in the accounts they send over, I will not presume to decide. But if the former supposition be the true one,—if they have been so long really acting over and over again in their own persons such a drama, it must be allowed that they deserve to be characterized as they have been in the description given of certain European nations: "An Englishman," it has been said, "is never happy but when he is miserable; a Scotchman is never at home but when he is abroad; an Irishman is never at peace but when he is fighting; a Spaniard is never at liberty but when he is enslaved; and a Frenchman is never settled but when he is engaged in a revolution."

POSTSCRIPT TO THE
TWELFTH EDITION.

"Time" says the proverb, "rings Truth to light." But the process is gradual and slow. The debt is paid, as it were, by instalments. It is only bit by bit, and at considerable intervals, that Truth comes forth as the morning twilight to dispel the mists of fiction.

It is above forty years that men have been debating the question:—Who were the parties that burned the city of Moscow?—without ever thinking of the preliminary question, whether it ever was burnt at all. And now at length we learn that it never was.

The following extract from a New Orleans paper contains the information obtained by an American traveller—one of that great nation whose accuracy as to facts is so well known— who visited the spot.

Incidents of Travel – City of Moscow

Senator Douglas is said to have made the discovery, while travelling in Russia, that the city of Moscow was never burned! The following statement of the matter is from the Muscatine (Iowa) Inquirer:

"Coming on the boat, a few days ago, we happened to fall in company with Senator

Douglas, who came on board at Quincy, on his way to Warsaw. In the course of a very interesting account of his travels in Russia, much of which has been published by letter-writers, he stated a fact which has never yet been published, but which startlingly contradicts the historical relation of one of the most extraordinary events that ever fell to the lot of history to record. For this reason the Judge said he felt a delicacy in making the assertion, that the city of Moscow was never burned!

"He said, that previous to his arrival at Moscow, he had several disputes with his guide as to the burning of the city, the guide declaring that it never occurred, and seeming to be nettled at Mr. Douglas's persistency in his opinion; but, on examining the fire-marks around the city, and the city itself, he became satisfied that the guide was correct.

"The statement goes on to set forth that the antiquity of the architectural city—particularly of its 'six hundred first-class churches,' stretching through ante-Napoleonic ages to Pagan times, and showing the handiwork of different nations of History—demonstrates that the city never was burned down (or up)."

The Inquirer adds:

"The Kremlin is a space of several hundred acres, in the heart of the city, in the shape of a flat iron, and is enclosed, by a wall of sixty feet high. Within this enclosure is the most magnificent palace in Europe, recently built, but constructed over an ancient palace, which remains, thus enclosed, whole and perfect, with all its windows, etc.

"Near the Kremlin, surrounded by a wall, is a Chinese town, appearing to be several hundred years old, still occupied by descendants of the original settlers.

"The circumstances which gave rise to the errors concerning the burning of Moscow, were these:—It is a city of four hundred and fifty thousand inhabitants, in circular form, occupying a large space, five miles across. There the winters are six months long, and the custom was, and still is, to lay up supplies of provisions and wood to last six months of severe cold weather. To prevent these gigantic supplies from encumbering the heart of the city, and yet render them as convenient as practicable to every locality, a row of wood houses was constructed to circle completely round the city, and outside of these was a row of granaries, and in these were deposited the whole of the supplies. Napoleon had entered the city with his army, and was himself occupying the palace of the Kremlin, when, one night, by order of the

Russian governor, every wood house and every granary simultaneously burst into a blaze. All efforts to extinguish them were vain, and Napoleon found himself compelled to march his army through the fire. Retiring to an eminence he saw the whole city enveloped in vast sheets of flame, and clouds of smoke, and apparently all on fire. And far as he was concerned it might as well have been, for though houses enough were left to supply every soldier with a room, yet without provisions or fuel, and a Russian army to cut off supplies, he and his army could not subsist there. During the fire some houses were probably burnt, but the city was not. In the Kremlin a magazine blew up, cracking the church of Ivan more than a hundred feet up, but setting nothing on fire.

"Mr. Douglas saw the fire-marks around the city, where wood houses and granaries for winter supplies now stand as of old; but there appears no marks of conflagration within the city."

Any wary sceptic, indeed, might have found much ground for doubt in the very accounts themselves that were given of the conflagration. For, the Russians have always denied that *they* burned it; and the French equally disclaimed the act. Each of the two parties between whom the accusation lay, strenuously denied it. And it must be acknowledged that each had very strong presumptions of innocence to urge. It was certainly most *unlikely* that the Russians should themselves destroy their ancient and venerable capital; and that, too, when they were boasting of having just gained a great victory at Borodino over an army which, therefore, they might hope to defeat again, and to drive out of their city. And it was no less unlikely that the French should burn down a city of which they had possession, and which afforded shelter and refreshment to their troops. This would have been one of the most improbable circumstances of that most improbable (supposed) campaign. To add to the marvel, we are told that the French army nevertheless waited for five weeks, without any object, amid the ashes of this destroyed city, just at the approach, of winter, and as if on purpose to be overtaken and destroyed by snows and frost!

However, all the difficulties of the question whether any of these things took place at all, were by most persons overlooked, because the question itself never occurred to them, in their eagerness to decide *who* it was that burned the city. And at length it comes out that the answer is, Nobody!

THE END.

POSTSCRIPT.

With respect to the foregoing arguments, it has been asserted (though without even any attempt at proof) that they go to prove that the Bible-narratives contain nothing more miraculous than the received accounts of Napoleon Buonapartè. And this is indeed true, if we use the word "*miraculous*" in the very unusual sense in which Hume (as is pointed out in the foregoing pages) has employed it; to signify simply "*improbable*;" an abuse of language on which his argument mainly depends.

It is indeed shown, that there are at least as many and as great *improbabilities* in the history of Buonapartè as in any of the Scripture-narratives; and that as plausible objections,—if not more so,—may be brought against the one history as the other.

But taking words in their ordinary, established sense, the assertion is manifestly the opposite of the truth. For, any one who does,—in spite of all the improbabilities,—*believe* the truth of *both* histories, is, evidently, a believer in miracles; since he believes two narratives, one of which is *not* miraculous, while the other is. The history of Buonapartè contains—though much that is very improbable—nothing that is to be called, according to the established use of language, miraculous. And the Scriptures contain, as an *essential* part of their narrative, *Miracles*, properly so called.

To talk of believing the Bible, all *except the Miracles*, would be like professing to believe the accounts of Buonapartè, *except* only his commanding armies, and having been at Elba and at Saint Helena.

One cannot doubt that in the course of the *forty years* that this little Work has been before the Public, some real, valid refutation of the argument would have been adduced, if any such could have been devised.

1860.

INDEX

www.ingramcontent.com/pod-product-compliance
Lightning Source LLC
Chambersburg PA
CBHW071625040426
42452CB00009B/1494

A Note From Rick Renner

I am on a personal quest to see a "revival of the Bible" so people can establish their lives on a firm foundation that will stand strong and endure the test as end-time storm winds begin to intensify.

In order to experience a revival of the Bible in your personal life, it is important to take time each day to read, receive, and apply its truths to your life. James tells us that if we will continue in the perfect law of liberty — refusing to be forgetful hearers, but determined to be doers — we will be blessed in our ways. As you watch or listen to the programs in this series and work through this corresponding study guide, I trust you will search the Scriptures and allow the Holy Spirit to help you hear something new from God's Word that applies specifically to your life. I encourage you to be a doer of the Word He reveals to you. Whatever the cost, I assure you — it will be worth it.

> Thy words were found, and I did eat them;
> and thy word was unto me the joy and rejoicing of mine heart:
> for I am called by thy name, O Lord God of hosts.
> — Jeremiah 15:16

Your brother and friend in Jesus Christ,

Rick Renner

Unless otherwise indicated, all scripture quotations are taken from the *King James Version* of the Bible.

Scripture quotations marked (*AMPC*) are taken from the *Amplified® Bible, Classic Edition*. Copyright © 1954, 1958, 1962, 1964, 1965, 1987 by The Lockman Foundation. Used by permission. **www.Lockman.org**.

Scripture quotations marked (*NKJV*) are taken from the *New King James Version®*. Copyright © 1982 by Thomas Nelson. Used by permission. All rights reserved.

Scripture quotations marked (*NLT*) are taken from the Holy Bible, *New Living Translation*, copyright © 1996, 2004, 2015 by Tyndale House Foundation. Used by permission of Tyndale House Publishers, Inc., Carol Stream, Illinois 60188. All rights reserved.

Scripture quotations marked (*RIV*) are taken from *Renner Interpretive Version*. Copyright © 2021 by Rick Renner.

How To Know the Difference Between True and False Prophets

Copyright © 2024 by Rick Renner
1814 W. Tacoma St.
Broken Arrow, OK 74012-1406

Published by Rick Renner Ministries
www.renner.org

ISBN 13: 978-1-6675-1126-9

ISBN 13 eBook: 978-1-6675-1127-6

All rights reserved. No portion of this book may be reproduced or transmitted in any form or by any means — electronic, mechanical, photocopy, recording, scanning, or other — except for brief quotations in critical reviews or articles, without the prior written permission of the Publisher.

Rick Renner's guest during this series is Joseph Z, founder of Z Ministries. Joseph is an international prophetic voice who builds lives by the Word of God in the church, government, and marketplace. He and his wife Heather currently reside in Colorado Springs, CO, with their two children. For more information, visit **josephz.com**.